Reptile Body Parts

Clare Lewis

© 2016 Heinemann-Raintree
an imprint of Capstone Global Library, LLC
Chicago, Illinois

To contact Capstone Global Library please call 800-747-4992, or visit our web site www.capstonepub.com

Edited by Helen Cox Cannons and Shelly Lyons
Designed by Steve Mead
Picture research by Svetlana Zhurkin
Production by Victoria Fitzgerald
Originated by Capstone Global Library Ltd
Printed and bound in China by Leo Paper Products Ltd

19 18 17 16 15
10 9 8 7 6 5 4 3 2 1

Library of Congress Cataloging-in-Publication Data
Lewis, Clare, 1976- author.
  Reptile body parts / Clare Lewis.
     pages cm.—(Animal body parts)
Includes bibliographical references and index.
  ISBN 978-1-4846-2554-5 (hb)—ISBN 978-1-4846-2561-3 (pb)—ISBN 978-1-4846-2575-0 (ebook) 1. Reptiles—Anatomy—Juvenile literature. I. Title.

QL669.L66 2016
597.9—dc23   2014044030

This book has been officially leveled by using the F&P Text Level Gradient™ Leveling System.

Acknowledgments
We would like to thank the following for permission to reproduce photographs: Dreamstime: Elena Zarubina, 10, John Wollwerth, 6, Joshkho, cover (top left), Mgkuijpers, 14; iStockphoto: KonArt, back cover (right), 16, 23; Newscom: Photoshot/NHPA/Dave Watts, 17, Photoshot/NHPA/Reinhard Dirscherl, 20; Shutterstock: Anna Azimi, 18, Audrey Snider-Bell, 5, 23, Cathy Keifer, 8, Dmytro Pylypenko, 15, Evgeny Tsapov, cover (top middle), Giampaolo Cianella, 22 (top), Matt Jeppson, 21, NagyDodo, cover (top right), pattyphotoart, 11, Peter Waters, 22 (middle), photoiconix, cover (bottom), reptiles4all, 13, 23, Rich Carey, 12, 23, Rolf E. Staerk, back cover (left), 9, Sebastian Duda, 7, Willie Davis, 4, 23, Yuriy V. Kuzmenko, 22 (bottom); SuperStock: Scubazoo, 19.

We would like to thank Michael Bright for his invaluable help in the preparation of this book.

Contents

Some words are shown in bold, **like this**. You can find out what they mean by looking in the glossary.

What Is a Reptile?

Reptiles are "**cold-blooded**" animals. Most reptiles have scales or shells, and they lay eggs.

Snakes and turtles are reptiles.

Reptiles do not all look the same. Their bodies can be very different from each other.

Let's take a look at their body parts.

Eyes

Reptiles have two eyes. This alligator's eyes are on top of its head.

The alligator can watch for **prey** while its body is hidden underwater.

Chameleons can move each eye by itself.

They can look in two directions at the same time!

Ears and Noses

ear hole

Most reptiles use their bodies to sense what is happening around them. They can also hear. But their ears are tiny.

This gecko has small ear holes.

nostrils

Reptiles have noses with two nostrils for breathing and smelling.

Turtles, like this one, have nostrils. They have a very good sense of smell for finding food.

Mouths and Tongues

Snakes can open their mouths very wide. They cannot chew or tear their food. Instead, they swallow it whole.

This huge snake can even swallow a goat!

Crocodiles sometimes lie quietly with their mouths wide open. This helps them to cool down.

Teeth

Crocodiles have sharp teeth for catching **prey**. Most turtles have beaks but no teeth.

This green sea turtle uses its beak to eat seaweed and sea grasses.

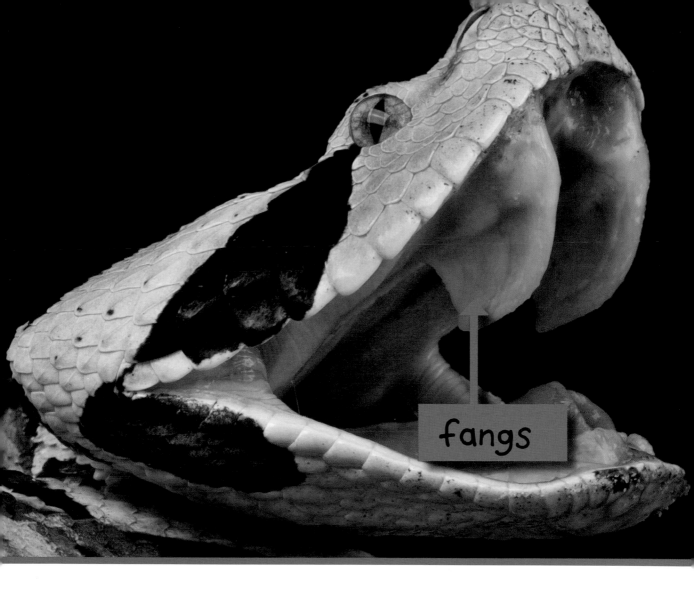

fangs

Venomous snakes, such as this viper, have special teeth called fangs. "Venomous" means that these snakes have **venom**. Venom is a liquid poison that runs through the snake's fangs into its prey and kills it.

Legs and Feet

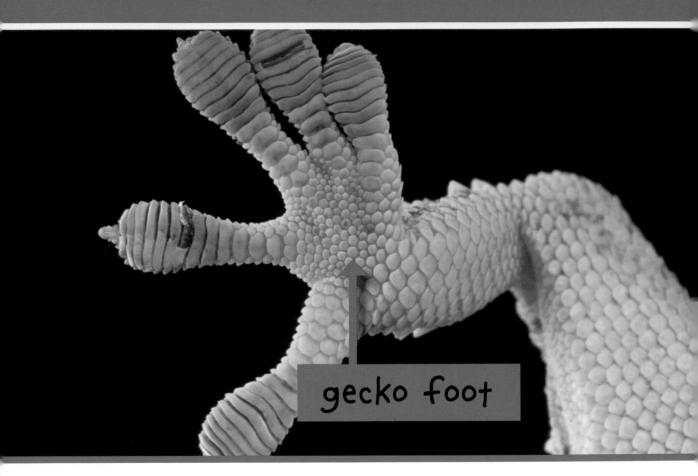

gecko foot

Chameleons have special toes that help them grip branches and climb trees.

Geckoes have sticky feet. They can even walk upside down!

Snakes and some lizards have no legs.
They use their strong muscles to pull
themselves along the ground.

Spines and Frills

Some lizards, such as this thorny dragon, have **spines** on their backs. Spines help protect them from **predators**.

frill

This Australian frilled lizard has a frill around its neck. The frill helps the lizard scare away predators.

Shells

Most turtles and tortoises have hard shells. This protects them from **predators**.

This giant tortoise has pulled its head into its shell for safety.

The leatherback turtle's tough shell is soft.
It is made of bony plates that fit together.
Its shell is teardrop shaped to help it
swim as fast as possible.

Tails

Most reptiles have tails. Rattlesnakes rattle their tails to warn off **predators**.

Crocodiles use their powerful tails to swim quickly through water.

Some small lizards can lose their tails if they are being attacked.

The tail drops off and the lizard runs away. Another tail will grow in its place.

Totally Amazing Reptile Body Parts!

Chameleons use their tails to hang on to branches. Not many reptiles have twisty tails like this!

This skink has a bright-blue tongue. The skink sticks out its tongue to scare away **predators**.

A Komodo dragon is the biggest lizard. Komodo dragons have powerful claws on their feet for attacking **prey**.

Glossary

cold-blooded animals that get their body temperature from the air around them. Most reptiles can get warm only by sitting in the sun.

predator animal that hunts other animals for food

prey animal that is hunted by another animal

spine sharp, pointed part that sticks out from some animals' bodies

venom liquid poison produced by some animals. Venom is put into other animals through a bite or sting.

Find Out More

Books

Royston, Angela. *Reptiles* (Animal Classifications). Chicago: Heinemann Library, 2015.

Stille, Darlene R. *The Life Cycle of Reptiles* (Life Cycles). Chicago: Heinemann Library, 2012.

Web sites

Facthound offers a safe, fun way to find Internet sites related to this book. All of the sites on Facthound have been researched by our staff.

Here's all you do:
Visit www.facthound.com
Type in this code: 9781484625545

Index